INTRODUCTION

Butterflies and moths belong to the second largest order of insects (next to beetles) with approximately 170,000 species worldwide. All have two pairs of wings covered with overlapping layers of fine scales. They feed by uncoiling a long feeding tube (proboscis) and sucking nutrients from flowers, puddles, etc. When not in use, the tube is coiled under the head.

The two groups differ in several ways:

BUTTERFLIES
- Active by day
- Brightly colored
- Thin body
- Rests with wings held erect over its back
- Antennae are thin and thickened at the tip

MOTHS
- Active at night
- Most are dull-colored
- Stout body
- Rests with wings folded, tent-like, over its back
- Antennae are usually thicker and often feathery

All butterflies and moths have a complex life cycle consisting of four developmental stages.

1. **EGGS** – Eggs are laid singly or in clusters on vegetation or on the ground. One or more clutches of eggs may be laid each year.

2. **CATERPILLARS (LARVAE)** – These worm-like creatures hatch from eggs and feed primarily on plants (often on the host plant on which the eggs were laid). As they grow, larvae shed their skin periodically.

3. **PUPAE** – Pupae are the "cases" within which caterpillars transform into adults. The pupa of a butterfly is known as a chrysalis; those of moths are called cocoons. In cooler regions, pupae often overwinter before maturing into butterflies or moths.

4. **ADULT** – Butterflies/moths emerge from pupae to feed and breed.

ATTRACTING BUTTERFLIES TO YOUR YARD

1. **Food** – Almost all butterfly caterpillars eat plants; adult butterflies feed almost exclusively on plant nectar. Your local garden shop, library and bookstore will have information on which plants attract specific species.

2. **Water** – Soak the soil in your garden or sandy areas to create puddles. These provide a source of water and minerals.

3. **Rocks** – Put large flat rocks in sunny areas. Butterflies will gather there to spread their wings and warm up.

4. **Brush** – Small brush piles and hollow logs provide ideal places for butterflies to lay their eggs and hibernate over the winter.

Most illustrations show the upper wings of males unless otherwise noted. The measurements denote the wingspan of species. Note that wing shape differs in flight and at rest. Illustrations are not to scale.

Waterford Press produces reference guides that introduce novices to nature, science, outdoor recreation and survival. Product information is featured on the website:
www.waterfordpress.com

Text and illustrations © 2020 by Waterford Press Inc. All rights reserved. Cover image © Shutterstock. To order, call 800-434-2555. For permissions, or to share comments, or to order in bulk quantities, call 800-434-2555 or e-mail editor@waterfordpress.com. For information on custom-published products, call 800-434-2555 or e-mail info@waterfordpress.com.

ISBN 978-1-62005-443-7

$7.95 U.S.

Made in the USA

206002

ARIZONA BUTTERFLIES & POLLINATORS

A Folding Pocket Guide to Familiar Species

SWALLOWTAILS & ALLIES

This family includes the largest butterfly species. Most are colorful and have a tail-like projection on each hindwing.

Pipevine Swallowtail
Battus philenor
To 3.5 in. (9 cm)
Note white crescent-shaped marks on outer edge of hindwings.

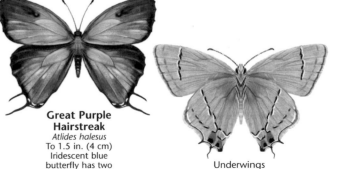

Giant Swallowtail
Papilio cresphontes
To 6 in. (15 cm)
One of the largest North American butterflies.

Old World Swallowtail
Papilio machaon
To 2.5 in. (6 cm)

Indra Swallowtail
Papilio indra
To 3 in. (8 cm)

Black Swallowtail
Papilio polyxenes
To 4 in. (10 cm)

Two-tailed Swallowtail
Papilio multicaudatus
To 5 in. (13 cm)
Note two tails on each hindwing.
Arizona's state insect.

Western Tiger Swallowtail
Papilio rutulus
To 4 in. (10 cm)

Anise Swallowtail
Papilio zelicaon
To 3 in. (8 cm)

WHITES & SULPHURS

White and yellow/orange butterflies are among the first to appear in spring.

Desert Orangetip
Anthocharis cethura
To 1.5 in. (4 cm)

Cabbage White
Pieris rapae
To 2 in. (5 cm)
One of the most common butterflies. Feeds on cabbage leaves and wild mustards.

Orange Sulphur
Colias eurytheme
To 2.5 in. (6 cm)
Gold-orange butterfly has prominent forewing spot.

Sleepy Orange
Eurema nicippe
To 2 in. (5 cm)
Slow flier is very common in the southern states.

Checkered White
Pontia protodice
To 1.75 in. (4.5 cm)

Southern Dogface
Zerene cesonia
To 2.5 in. (6 cm)
Note poodle-head pattern on forewings.

Clouded Sulphur
Colias philodice
To 2 in. (5 cm)
Note wing spots and dark margin to wings. Common in open areas and along roadsides.

Cloudless Sulphur
Phoebis sennae
To 3 in. (8 cm)
Common in open areas.

GOSSAMER-WINGED BUTTERFLIES

This family of small bluish or coppery butterflies often has small, hair-like tails on its hindwings. Most rest with their wings folded and underwings exposed.

Great Purple Hairstreak
Atlides halesus
To 1.5 in. (4 cm)
Iridescent blue butterfly has two black tails on each hindwing.

Underwings

Gray Hairstreak
Strymon melinus
To 1.25 in. (3.2 cm)
Uppenwings are brownish. Orange marks are visible from both sides.

Brown Elfin
Incisalia augustinus
To 1 in. (3 cm)

Spring Azure
Celastrina ladon
To 1.25 in. (3.2 cm)
One of the earliest spring butterflies.

Arizona Hairstreak
Erora quaderna
To 1 in. (3 cm)

Juniper Hairstreak
Mitoura siva
To 1 in. (3 cm)

Western Pygmy Blue
Brephidium exilis
To .75 in. (2 cm)
White-fringed brown butterfly is purplish near the body. Underwings have 4–6 iridescent spots.

Marine Blue
Leptotes marina
To 1 in. (3 cm)

SKIPPERS

Named for their fast, bouncing flight, skippers have distinctive antennae that end in curved clubs.

Yucca Giant Skipper
Megathymus yuccae
To 3 in. (8 cm)

Underwings

Silver-spotted Skipper
Epargyreus clarus
To 2.5 in. (6 cm)
Has a large, irregular silver patch on the underside of its hindwings. Patch is absent on the forewings.

Arizona Skipper
Codatractus arizonensis
To 2 in. (5 cm)

Orange Skipperling
Copaeodes aurantiaca
To 1 in. (3 cm)

Apache Skipper
Hesperia woodgatei
To 1.5 in. (4 cm)

Arizona Powdered Skipper
Systasea zampa
To 1.5 in. (4 cm)

Common Sootywing
Pholisora catullus
To 1.25 in. (3.2 cm)

Pahaska Skipper
Hesperia pahaska
To 1.5 in. (4 cm)

This family is named for its small forelegs that they use to "taste" food.

California Sister
Adelpha californica
To 3.5 in. (9 cm)

Viceroy
Limenitis archippus
To 3.5 in. (9 cm)
Told from similar Monarch
by its smaller size and
the thin, black band
on its hindwings.

Hackberry Emperor
Asterocampa celtis
To 2.5 in. (6 cm)
Is gray-brown to orange.

Mourning Cloak
Nymphalis antiopa
To 3.5 in. (9 cm)

Weidemeyer's Admiral
Limenitis weidemeyerii
To 3.5 in. (9 cm)

Common Ringlet
Coenonympha tullia
To 1.5 in. (4 cm)

Mormon Metalmark
Apodemia mormo
To 1.25 in. (3.2 cm)
Brushfoot-like species
belongs to the
Metalmark family.

Field Crescentspot
Phyciodes campestris
To 1.5 in. (4 cm)

Red-spotted Purple
Limenitis arthemis astyanax
To 3.5 in. (9 cm)

Sagebrush Checkerspot
Chlosyne acastus
To 2 in. (5 cm)

Canyonland Satyr
Cyllopsis pertepida
To 1.75 in. (4.5 cm)

Queen
Danaus gilippus
To 3.5 in. (9 cm)
Rich, brown-orange wings are
finely spotted with white dots.

Monarch
Danaus plexippus
To 4 in. (10 cm)
Note rows of white
spots on edges of wings.
Annual migration covers
thousands of miles.

Variegated Fritillary
Euptoieta claudia
To 2.5 in. (6 cm)

Buckeye
Junonia coenia
To 2.5 in. (6 cm)
Note orange wing
bars on forewings and 8
distinct "eyespots."

Gulf Fritillary
Agraulis vanillae
To 3 in. (8 cm)
Underwings are covered
with metallic silver spots.

Satyr Anglewing
Polygonia satyrus
To 2 in. (5 cm)

Red Admiral
Vanessa atalanta
To 2.5 in. (6 cm)
Dark butterfly has
prominent orange
bars on forewings and
border of hindwings.

Mylitta Crescentspot
Phyciodes mylitta
To 1.5 in. (4 cm)

Atlantis Fritillary
Speyeria atlantis
To 2.5 in. (6 cm)
Underwings are
silver-spotted.

West Coast Lady
Vanessa annabella
To 2 in. (5 cm)

Painted Lady
Vanessa cardui
To 2.5 in. (6 cm)
Tip of forewing is dark
with white spots.

American Snout
Libytheana carinenta
To 2 in. (5 cm)
"Snout" is formed
from projecting mouth
parts which enclose its
coiled proboscis.

Variable Checkerspot
Euphydryas chalcedona
To 2 in. (5 cm)
Black caterpillar
has orange stripes.

Cecrops-eyed Silkmoth
Automeris cecrops
To 4 in. (10 cm)

Western Sheep Moth
Hemileuca eglanterina
To 3 in. (8 cm)
Common in pastures
and meadows.

Acrea Moth
Estigmene acraea
To 2 in. (5 cm)

White-lined Sphinx
Hyles lineata
To 3.5 in. (9 cm)
Active at all hours,
it hovers like a
hummingbird.

Juno Buckmoth
Hemileuca juno
To 3 in. (8 cm)

Black Witch Moth
Ascalapha odorata
To 6 in. (15 cm)

Five-spotted Hawk Moth
Manduca quinquemaculata
To 5.5 in. (14 cm)
Agricultural pest feeds
on tomato, potato and
tobacco plants. Caterpillar
has a large horn at its rear.

Eyed Sphinx
Smerinthus cerisyi
To 3 in. (8 cm)

About 75% of the crop plants grown worldwide depend on pollinators – bees, butterflies, birds, bats and other animals – for fertilization and reproduction. Although some species of plants are pollinated by the wind and water, the vast majority (almost 90%) need the help of animals to act as pollinating agents. More than 1,000 of the world's most important foods, beverages and medicines are derived from plants that require pollination by animals.

Pollinating animals worldwide are threatened due to loss of habitat, introduced and invasive species, pesticides, diseases and parasites.

Bees, Wasps & Flies

North America is home to approximately 4,000 species of bees. Of these, the most important crop pollinators are wild native honey bees and managed colonies of European honey bees. Other important flying insects include bumble bees, mason bees, carpenter bees, wasps and numerous flies. With honey bee populations in huge decline due to certain illnesses and habitat loss, this can have a huge impact on food production in North America.

HONEY BEE ANATOMY

Beetles

The living jewels of the bug world, beetles are the dominant life group on the earth with about 400,000 species found in all habitats except the polar regions and the oceans. They are invaluable to ecosystems as both pollinators and scavengers, feeding on dead animals and fallen trees to recycle nutrients back into the soil. Some, however, are serious pests and cause great harm to living plants (trees, crops). Learn to recognize the good from the bad and involve your local land management and pest control resources to mitigate the spread of harmful beetles.

BEETLE ANATOMY

Birds, Bats & Other Animals

More than 50 species of North American birds occasionally feed on plant nectar and blossoms, but it is the primary food source for hummingbirds and orioles. Sugar water feeders are a good way to supplement the energy of nectar drinkers, but it is far better to plant flowers and shrubs that provide native sources of nutrient-rich nectar. While very common in tropical climates around the world, only three species of nectar-feeding bats are found in the southwestern U.S. They are important pollinators of desert plants including large cacti (organ pipe, saguaro), agaves and century plants. Rodents, lizards and small mammals like mice also pollinate plants when feeding on their nectar and flower heads.

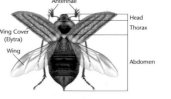

Black-chinned Hummingbird

Long-nosed Bat

Attracting Bees & Other Pollinators

- Recognize the pollinators in your area and plant gardens to support the larvae and adults of different species.
- Cultivate native pollen and nectar-producing plants that bloom at different times throughout the growing season. Ensure the species you select will thrive with the amount of sunshine and moisture at the site. Reduce/eliminate use of pesticides. If you use any type of repellent, ensure it is organic and pesticide-free.
- The plants that attract birds, butterflies and moths for pollination most commonly have bright red, orange or yellow flowers with very little scent. Butterflies prefer flat-topped "cluster" flowers. Hummingbirds prefer tube or funnel-shaped flowers.
- Create areas, out of the sun, where pollinators can rest and avoid predation while foraging.
- Supply water for both drinking and bathing. Create shallow puddles for bees and butterflies.
- Create nesting boxes or brushy areas that provide protection from predation and are suitable for pollinators to raise their young.
- Learn to recognize the good and bad garden bugs.

Giant Swallowtail

Black Swallowtail

Skipper

Pipevine Swallowtail

Gulf Fritillary

Monarch

Cabbage White

Painted Lady

Mourning Cloak

Viceroy

Red-spotted Purple

Buckeye

White-lined Sphinx

Five-spotted Hawk Moth